Foul Play

John Goodwin

Published in association with
The Basic Skills Agency

Hodder Murray

A MEMBER OF THE HODDER HEADLINE GROUP

Hodder Headline's policy is to use papers that are natural, renewable and recyclable products and made from wood grown in sustainable forests. The logging and manufacturing processes are expected to conform to the environmental regulations of the country of origin.

Orders: please contact Bookpoint Ltd, 130 Milton Park, Abingdon, Oxon OX14 4SB. Telephone: (44) 01235 827720. Fax: (44) 01235 400454. Lines are open from 9.00am to 5.00pm, Monday to Saturday, with a 24-hour message answering service.
Visit our website at www.hoddereducation.co.uk

First published in the Livewire series in 2000 and first published in the Hodder Reading Project series in 2006 by Hodder Murray, an imprint of Hodder Education, a member of the Hodder Headline Group, 338 Euston Road, London NW1 3BH.

Impression number   10 9 8 7 6 5 4
Year   2011 2010 2009 2008 2007

Cover photo: Referee © Banana Stock / Alamy.
Internal artwork © Oxford Designers and Illustrators.
Typeset by Transet Ltd, Coventry, England.
Printed in Great Britain by CPI, Bath.

A catalogue record for this title is available from the British Library

ISBN-10: 0 340 91569 2
ISBN-13: 978 0340 915 691

Contents

1

Trouble

Kick the ball.
Kick it hard. Kick it straight.
Kick it at the third brick in the wall.
Think the brick is one of your forwards.
Pass it to the brick with the side
of your foot. Don't toe-end it.

The brick passes it back.
A one-two pass.
Control it and then off down the wing.
Side step one.
Side step two and the goal is in sight.
Steady now … take aim.
Hit the goal below the drain pipe.

Now for a bit of heading.
Throw the ball up in the air.
Head straight through the ball.
Don't close your eyes.
Hit it with your forehead.
I hate this bit. Really hate it.

'Jump!' I tell myself.
'Come on, Jamie. Just go for it.'
Only I miss the ball and fall in a heap.
A nasty laugh comes from the back
of the garages.
I'd know that laugh anywhere.
'Come on, Spider. Go for it,'
says a mocking voice.

Only Chocka and some of his mates
call me Spider.
He's the biggest thug in our school.
Big mouth and bigger fists.
You don't argue with Chocka.

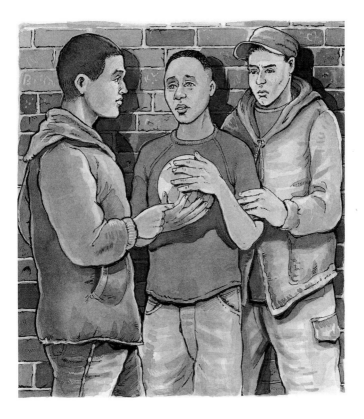

It was time to make a move.
It was time to grab the football
and sprint away from the bit of waste
ground behind the supermarket.
I had to get away fast,
but I reckoned without Dim Dezzy,
Chocka's skinny mate.

Next thing I know,
Dezzy steps out in front of me.
He grabs the ball out of my hands
and legs it over the supermarket wall.
That was a top class leather ball,
none of your cheap plastic rubbish,
but I knew I could wave it goodbye.

'Spider … Spider's lost his ball,'
they shouted,
from behind the supermarket wall.

All I could do was head off home
with my head low.
Chocka and his mates
had won another victory.

2

Free Kick

I ran onto the football pitch
as fast as I could.
I'd show them this time.
I wasn't going to let it get to me.
Chocka wasn't going to stop me
having a decent game of footie.

I did a sprint up and down the pitch
while the rest of the class
were still in the changing room.

Then the rest came out.
I heard Chocka laughing
and shouting out,
'Spider … Spider man … see him fly.'
He wasn't that clever.
Spiders can't fly but they catch flies.
He'd better remember that.

Mr Jensen picked two teams.
I finished up on the same team
as Big Mouth and his dim mate.
They both started to moan.
'Oh no … he's a useless spider.
We don't want him.
Can't he play for the other team?'

But Mr Jensen wasn't having any of it.
'He's in your team.
Any more from you two
and you'll get the red card.'

We kicked off.
I ran up the field to play striker.
I found myself a bit of space
and looked at their goalie, Winston.
He wasn't that good.
A hard low shot would beat him.

The ball was being played up near me.
'Pass!' I shouted. 'Pass it … pass it!'
It was as if I was on a different planet.
No pass came.
Nobody came near me.
We had three attacks on goal
and failed all of them.
I didn't get one pass.

Mr Big Mouth lost the ball each time.
It was like there was nobody
in the team but him. What a wally –
big mouth, big feet and no brain.

At last we got a free kick.
It was close enough to have a shot at goal.
Mr Jensen blew his whistle hard.
'Free kick. You take it, Jamie,' he said.
He placed the ball on the ground.

'Not him!' shouted Chocka.
'He can't kick his way out of
a bag of chips.'

Mr Jensen ignored him.
I looked at the ball and up to the goal.
A good hard low shot on target.
That was what I had to do.

Then I heard Dezzy whispering,
'Spider ... Spider man.'

I admit it got to me. I couldn't block it.
There was no hard low shot.
No shot at all.

My foot hit the ground in front of the ball.
It just trickled a few centimetres forward.
Then it stopped.

I could hear booing
from the rest of the team.
Mr Jensen blew his whistle hard.
'Half-time. Change ends
and cut out that booing.'

3

A Favour

Smack! A hand grabbed at me.
The hand was on my shoulder
and pulling me back.
I stopped dead in my tracks.
I just froze. Then there was laughing.

'Where do spiders come from?'
said Chocka from behind my back.
'Smelly little holes,'
said Dezzy next to him.
'Cos they're smelly little creatures.
They can't kick their way out of
a bag of chips,' said Chocka,
whispering really close in my ear.

'They're losers,' said Dezzy.
'Don't ever have them on your team,'
said Chocka.

Then he pulled hard
and swung me round to face him.
'I bet you want your ball back,' he said.
I just kept quiet,
but he wouldn't let it rest.
'Come on …
do you want your football back?
Yes or no?'

I just looked at the ground.
'Spiders can't speak,' said Dezzy.
'They've got no tongues.'
Chocka got hold of my arm
and started twisting it.
'Let go … you're hurting,' I said.

He was still twisting it as he pulled me
down the street and round the back
of the supermarket.

Then he said, 'We are prepared
to do you a favour. Right?'

I looked him in the eyes.
There was no right about this,
not any bit of it.

'Me and Dez fancy
some smart new footie kit,' he said.
'New boots, Man U strip.
So we can look really cool.'
I nearly said that they could never
look cool.
But I said nothing.

'If you help us get that strip,
you get the ball back.
Easy as that,' he said.

Then he gave my arm an extra twist.
'That lock-up place down
the industrial estate's got some
really cool kit.
All you have to do is go in
and help yourself. Easy peasy.
You be down there tonight.
Half ten. OK?'

No, it wasn't OK. It wasn't.
I decided I wasn't going
anywhere near that place.
They could forget it.
I wasn't a thief.
Let them do their own dirty work.
If they wanted to break into the lock-up,
they could do it themselves.
I went home and watched football
on the telly.
That's where I'd be at half ten.
Taking it easy and watching telly.

4

The Lock-Up

It was pitch black.
So black you couldn't see your hand
in front of your face.

I cursed the blackness.
I cursed myself for being so stupid.
I said I was going to watch telly.
Yet here I was trying to steal football kit.
It was pathetic.

I moved forward a little.
My hands reached out in front of me.
They tried to grasp at anything before me.
A pile of kit,
a box stuffed with football boots,
shelves with bundles of football shirts.
Anything. They found … nothing.

I shuffled forward again.
Again I reached out in the blackness.
Again I found nothing.
I wanted to be out of it.
Only now I didn't know
which was the way out.
I was completely lost.
This way? That way? Which way?

From outside came voices.
'Spider.'
'Come on, Spider.'
'We're getting cold out here.'

I turned my head this way and that.
I tried to work out where the voices
were coming from,
so I could find my way out.
Let them stuff their stupid kit.
I was getting out of the lock-up.

I moved my foot. It hit something.
It was something big.
I reached out to try to touch it,
only I couldn't feel it.
Then my hands hit it.

It was big … and square and …
it was a box, a big cardboard box.
Perhaps it was full of football kit.
I could feel big flaps on top of the box.
I tried to pull one of the flaps.
It was stuck down. I pulled again.
Slowly, very slowly, the flap started to …

Red lights flashing.
Bright red lights flashing.
An alarm was ringing – loudly.

I ran. I ran like crazy,
out of the lock-up,
out through the industrial estate.
I ran empty-handed. I didn't look back.
I didn't stop till I got home.
Then I closed the door tight behind me.

5

Dirty Tricks

I waited for it all to happen.
Maybe the police would come round.
They didn't.

Maybe Chocka would kick my head in.
He didn't. It all went very quiet.

Then it began.

On Monday, pages were ripped out of
my school books.
Nobody saw it happen.

On Tuesday, somebody threw paint
all over our front door.
Nobody saw it happen.
On Wednesday, somebody slashed
the tyres on my bike.
Guess what? ... Nobody saw it happen.

Thursday was school football.
I tried to go sick.

'Can't play, Mr Jensen.'
'Why not, Jamie?'
'Bad leg, sir.'
'Have you got a sick note?'
'No, sir.'
'You know the rules.
No sick note, no excuse. Get changed.'

I knew something was going to happen.
It did. I turned my back for a few minutes
in the changing room
and my bag went missing.

'Mr Jensen … my bag is missing.'
'It can't be. Search the changing room.'
'I've searched it twice.
The bag had all my football kit in it, sir.'

Mr Jensen came into the changing room.
He looked at all the class.
'Jamie's bag has gone missing,' he said.
'Look in all your stuff … under the seats …
in the lockers. Let's see if we can find it.'

The changing room was searched,
but no bag was found.
Mr Jensen looked at the class again.

'If somebody has stolen Jamie's bag,
they are in big trouble.
The bag had all his football kit in it.
This may be a matter for the police.
If one of you here is a thief,
I want to know who it is.'

It went very quiet.

Mr Jensen was looking at the class.

'I am going to ask you one at a time
if you know anything about this.'

It was still silent.

He turned to face each boy in turn.

'Wayne?'

'No, sir.'

'Ravi?'

'No, sir.'

Mr Jensen came to face Chocka.

He called him by his real name.

'Paul?'

Chocka didn't move at all.

'No, sir,' he said.

I was getting angry.
Of course Chocka knew something about it.
The slashed tyres, the ripped books
and the wet paint.
Oh yes, Mr Big Mouth knew plenty
about all those.
He knew plenty about my missing kit,
but finding out the truth
was something else.

Mr Jensen reached Dezzy.
'Daniel?'
Dezzy looked guilty.
He started to bite his lip.
'Daniel … do you know anything
about this?'
Dezzy mumbled something.
'What was that?' asked Mr Jensen.
'No,' said Dezzy.
'Are you sure?'
Dezzy bit into his lip again.
It went very quiet.

Then suddenly Winston jumped up.
'It was Dezzy and Chocka!'
shouted Winston.
'They did it!'

Now Chocka got angry.
'You liar ... I never did anything.'
But Winston stood his ground.
'They did ... they did ... look!'

Winston pointed towards
the top of the locker.
Everybody's eyes looked up.

'I can't see anything,' said Mr Jensen.

'They hid his bag on top of the locker.
I saw them do it,' said Winston.

Mr Jensen climbed up on a bench.
He reached up high and pulled
out something.
It was covered with cobwebs.
He looked at me.
'Is this your bag, Jamie?'
'Yes, sir,' I said.
'Check it over.'

I opened the bag.
My boots, shirt and shorts were inside.
The shirt was stuffed into my boots.
As I pulled it out I could see
a big cut in it.
The shirt was ruined.
Mr Jensen took it out of my hands.

He looked straight at Chocka.
'Did you do this?' he asked.
'He did. He did. He's got it in for Jamie.
Him and Dezzy,' said Winston.
'Yes they have, sir. They have.
They always pick on him,'
shouted the rest of the class.

'Well they won't any longer,'
said Mr Jensen.
He turned to Chocka.
'Give me your football shirt, Paul,' he said.

'What for?' asked Chocka.

'Just do it,' said Mr Jensen.

The shiny new red football shirt
was handed over.

'There you are, Jamie,' he said
as he gave it to me.

'Wear it for the game.'

I put on the shirt.

It was big and came down to my knees.

'What am I going to play in?'
asked Chocka.

'You're not playing,' said Mr Jensen.

'And if you don't buy Jamie
a brand new shirt
by the end of the week,
the police will want to know why.'

6

Jamie's Big Chance

I'd won the battle of the football kit
but there was still a war going on –
a Chocka and Dezzy war.
They wouldn't take any prisoners.
They'd show no mercy.

I waited for them to strike again.
It could be any place and any time.
I had to be on my guard.

Two days later
there was a knock on our door.
I went to answer it. I opened the door.
There was nobody there.
I looked up the road both ways.
Nobody in sight.
'A Chocka trick,' I said to myself.

I went to shut the door.
Just as I did I saw something
on the ground.
I went to pick it up.
It was a football shirt.
A decent one.
There was no note on the shirt
but I knew who it was from.
'Maybe it's a trap,' I said to myself.
'Where will Chocka strike next?'

It wasn't Chocka that struck, but the flu.
It hit our school harder than a brick
thrown through a window.

Kids were sick everywhere.
Some puked up in assembly.
Some had to be taken home
in teachers' cars.
Chocka and Dezzy had it really bad.
I couldn't believe my luck.

Mr Jensen came to see me in Maths.
'Jamie,' he said, 'there's a school
football match tomorrow.
Because of the flu I'm short of players.
Can you play?'

Was this real? Could it be a wind-up?
Was it a very clever Chocka trick?
'Can you?' asked Mr Jensen again.
'Yes.'
'Good. The match is straight after school.
Just don't catch this flu.'
Then he left.
I couldn't think about Maths.
This was my big chance.

That night we had another knock
on the door.
I didn't open it straight away.
'Who is it?' I asked.
'It's Winston,' said a voice.
I looked through the letterbox
just to be sure it was him.
'We're both in the team tomorrow,'
he said.
'Do you fancy doing a bit of practice?'

We went to the waste ground,
behind the supermarket.
He'd brought a ball with him.
'I'm playing in goal,' he said.
'Kick a few at me.'

I kicked. He saved them.
I kicked hard.
I kicked low and high.
I kicked right and left. He saved the lot.
'You're doing brilliant,' I said.
'Yeah. But it's tomorrow that counts.'

Next we did some heading practice.
He threw the ball. I tried to head it.
Disaster. Worse than useless.
I missed every one.
'OK,' said Winston, 'relax, you're beaten
before your head comes anywhere near
the ball.'
Then he made me jump up in the air.
I jumped about until I was shattered.
'Just think you are heading that ball,'
he said. 'Tell yourself you can do it.'

While I was having a breather
we talked over football teams and players.
He was red hot on World Cup players
and teams.
Then he held the ball in his hands.
'Use your head. Knock the ball
out of my hands. Come on, go for it.'
I did. He began to throw the ball up.
Just a small throw. I had to head the ball.
I did. Most times anyway.
As Winston said, it's tomorrow that counts.

7

The Match

Who said tomorrow never comes?
It did, and so did the war.
After school I went to get changed
for the match.
Who was hanging
around the changing rooms?
You've guessed it.
Mr Big Fists.

I felt all my confidence vanish like
water rushing down a drain.
Dezzy was still away with the flu
but Chocka's mouth was big enough
for the both of them.

'They've got spiders playing
for the school now,' he said.
I could hear him shouting,
'Spider ... spider,' as I got changed.
I rushed out as quickly as I could.

The match began. I was in a blur.
It was all going too fast.
'Look out, Jamie.
Keep your eye on the ball!'
shouted Mr Jensen from the touchline.
All I could hear pounding in my ears was
'Spider ... spider.'

Somehow we kept it to 0–0.
Winston made some blinding saves.
If he hadn't been on top form
we'd have been 4–0 down.
'That practice worked,' he said to me.
'Yes.'
'Come on, Jamie. Relax.
Enjoy the game. You can do it.'

I knew he was trying to help
but I couldn't do it.
I was a useless spider.

'Come on, relax.
Don't go looking for trouble.
You can do it.'
I knew I had to get Chocka out of
my mind,
but there he was on the touchline
looking at me.

The second half began.
We kicked the ball upfield.
With a few short passes
we were near their goal.
'Brilliant play!' shouted Mr Jensen.
At last we won a corner.
'Go for it!' shouted Mr Jensen.
'Go for it!'
The corner was kicked high in the air.
It was coming down close to me.

This was a big chance.
I had to head the ball.
I tried to shut out Chocka.
I had to go for it.
'Now!' I said to myself. 'Go for it now!'

My feet were off the ground.
The ball was getting closer.
My head went towards the ball.
I don't know what happened next.
I think I closed my eyes.
I know my head hit the ball.

Down I fell in a heap.
I think the ball shot off my head
and hit the goal post.
I opened my eyes to see the ball
shoot out of play. Mr Jensen was cheering.
'Great header, Jamie. Brilliant.'

We hadn't scored a goal but it was a start.
Suddenly I felt in the game. I ran hard.
I went for the ball. I tackled their players.
I forgot about Chocka.
When I did look to see where he was,
he'd gone.

It was only a beginning.
I couldn't kid myself that Chocka
had gone forever. No way.
But maybe if I was lucky
I could find a way to handle him.
As Winston says,
'Don't go looking for trouble.
You can do it.'